SCOTLAND
THE · LIGHT · AND · THE · LAND

PHOTOGRAPHS · BY · COLIN · BAXTER

Salem House

SALEM NEW HAMPSHIRE

First published in the United States
by Salem House, 1985.
A member of the Merrimack Publishers' Circle,
47 Pelham Road, Salem NH 03079

Library of Congress Catalog Card Number
84-052247
ISBN 0 88162 086 6

© Copyright Colin Baxter 1985
Designed by Charles Miller Graphics
Words by R. A. James

Printed in Italy by
New Interlitho S.p.A., Milan

It is summer and a sweltering Scotland reaps a bumper harvest. Wave upon wave of ripe tourists sweeps in by road, rail and air to spill over ancient monuments and hills and mills and shops, inexorably drawn by images of loch and glen and ancient battleground. Though undoubtedly well armed with cameras, they will buy the cards and calendars and books proclaiming Scotland's Splendour, Scotland's Glory, Traditional Scotland or simply Scotland in Colour to reinforce their love affair with Scottishness.

This book is not about Scottishness but it is about Scotland: the country behind the myth, legend, history and romance, the inspiration for artist, patriot, Scot past, present and future. There is a timelessness about these photographs, which draw their strength from the elemental ingredients of sea and sky and land and light.

When Colin Baxter came to Scotland a few years ago, he recognized a photographer's dream when he saw one: an almost infinite source of pictures. These photographs have been taken over the past five years and represent a progress report so far. Although he has covered phenomenal distances, he knows there is so much still to be discovered and recorded.

Now photography has become the medium of the masses. The law of averages, combined with modern

technology, makes it inevitable that even the most cack-handed amateur photographer will achieve at least one masterpiece and the debate intensifies as to whether or not photography is really art. How can it be if anyone can do it? But what distinguishes the artist from other men is his ability to see and express, in whatever medium, aspects of human emotion or experience that would otherwise be overlooked: and to succeed in doing so over and over again.

Colin Baxter is modest about his achievements. He is even embarrassed by the ease with which he came by certain pictures–a question of being in the right place at the right time, with a camera–but if there is luck involved, he creates most of it. He is perpetually on the move, on the look-out for pictures and never without a camera. Journeys of exploration are planned with maps; locations noted for a revisit under specific conditions. But he is forever alert and responsive to those often momentary fusions of land and light that most of us have seen but all too rarely recognized and caught on films.

No book of Scottish landscape photographs can be definitive but in 'Scotland, the Light and the Land' Colin Baxter offers us a taste of the real thing and whets our appetite for more, much more to come.

Angus Ogilvy August, 1984

THE · BORDERS

6

iron
biting
brittle
whiting
dry
icing

FROST

trailing
westerly
the sun's
gold
an interlock
of land
and water

LOCH · TORRIDON

8

UPPER · CLYDE · VALLEY

9

OLD · MAN · OF · HOY

10

OLD · WINDOW

AYRSHIRE

12

ALLIGIN · SHUAS

13

APPLECROSS · FOREST.

14

sunset
breaking
into mountains
wave
on wave

LOCH · AWE

15

ISLE · OF · RAASAY

16

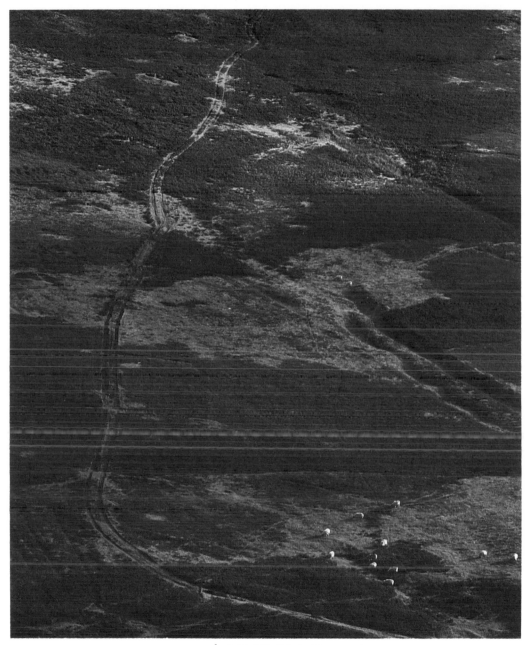

Leadhills

17

FORT · WILLIAM

CUNNINGHAME

BOATS

20

KINTYRE · PENINSULA

21

SANNA · BAY

22

shading
to brown
the ebb
and flow
of autumn
undulation

MELBOURNE · HILL

CRAWFORDJOHN

24

BEN · CRUACHAN

GOAT · FELL

LOCH · ARD · FOREST

27

PRESTONFIELD · GOLF · COURSE

FIRTH · OF · CLYDE

29

CRAIGNISH · POINT

shoaling
motionless
rock dorsals
chase
the sea

BEN · NEVIS

BROUGHTON · HEIGHTS

tree
figures
cloud
mountains
far
imaginings

MARSHLAND

33

EXPRESS

34

LOCH · LOMOND

35

DUSK · OVER · EDINBURGH

36

ST. · GILES · CATHEDRAL · & · SPIRES, · EDINBURGH

winter
pitted
the granite
blade

THE · LIGHT · AND · THE · LAND

BLACK · MOUNT

LOCH · BRACADALE

40

BEINN · EACH

41

COCKENZIE · POWER · STATION

42

EAST · COAST

43

MILK · BOTTLES

44

ISLE · OF · SKYE

45

FORESTRY

ABERLADY · SANDS

48

cropstrokes
scraping
brittle
colour
in the snow

BROOMY · LAW

LAMINGTON

LESMAHAGOW

50

SHIELDAIG

52

GLEN · ETIVE

53

WEST · COAST

54

WHITE · RIG · HILL

55

iron
oxide
yellow
ochre
burnt
umber
raw
sienna
tempera
mutantur

OLD · SHED

56

BRODICK · BAY

57

LOCH · LINNHE

LAMINGTON · POND

59

headlong
hung
the tumbled
precipice
of trees

BEINN · BHREAC

LOCH · DIABAIGAS · AIRDE

61

INNER · SOUND

62

LOWTHER · HILL

63

BROUGHTON · PLACE HARVEST

GREY · DOOR · AND · WINDOW

66

BOGHOUSE · FARM

ISLE · OF · ARRAN

68

blue hills
sweep
dusk
across
untroubled waters

BEINN · DAMH

stone
cold
shouldering
the sting
of winter's
whip

CLYDE · VALLEY

GLEN · LYON

POST · BOXES

CUILLIN · HILLS

GOSELAND · HILL

DUNEATON · VALLEY

75

sea
sand
grass
in shades
of wind

LOW · TIDE

76

ORKNEY CLIFFS

LOCH · EIL

78

SUMMER · EVENING

79

slopes
fingering
the mist
with trees

LOCH · ARD

WINTER · BORDERS

80

BEN · SHIELDAIG

82

GLEN CROE

83

COMMON · HILL

KINGAIRLOCH

85

flake
white
lead
grey
wind
bite
keel
spray

SILVER · SEA

MORNING · BORDERS

LOCH · VOIL

88

ROLLING · FIELDS

LIATHACH · TORRIDON

90

BROAD · HILL

TORRIDON · HILLS

92

TINTO · HILL

93